HAIR
THE MUSICAL
EASY PIANO

Published by
Wise Publications
14-15 Berners Street, London W1T 3LJ, UK.

Exclusive Distributors:
Music Sales Limited
Distribution Centre, Newmarket Road,
Bury St Edmunds, Suffolk IP33 3YB, UK.
Music Sales Corporation
180 Madison Avenue, 24th Floor, New York NY 10016, USA.
Music Sales Pty Limited
4th floor, Lisgar House, 30-32 Carrington Street,
Sydney, NSW 2000, Australia.

Order No. AM1010504
ISBN: 978-1-78305-944-7
This book © Copyright 2015 Wise Publications,
a division of Music Sales Limited.

Compiled and edited by Jenni Norey.
Music arranged by Alistair Watson.
Music processed by Paul Ewers Music Design.
Cover design by Tim Field.
Cover photograph of Marsha Hunt by
Mike McKeown/Daily Express/Hulton Archive/Getty Images.
Cover image from Fotolia.com

Printed in the EU.

Your Guarantee of Quality:

As publishers, we strive to produce every book
to the highest commercial standards.

This book has been carefully designed to minimise awkward
page turns and to make playing from it a real pleasure.

Particular care has been given to specifying acid-free, neutral-sized paper
made from pulps which have not been elemental chlorine bleached.
This pulp is from farmed sustainable forests and was produced
with special regard for the environment.

Throughout, the printing and binding have been planned to ensure a sturdy,
attractive publication which should give years of enjoyment.
If your copy fails to meet our high standards,
please inform us and we will gladly replace it.

www.musicsales.com

WISE PUBLICATIONS
part of The Music Sales Group
London / New York / Paris / Sydney / Copenhagen / Berlin / Madrid / Hong Kong / Tokyo

Aquarius

Words by James Rado & Gerome Ragni
Music by Galt MacDermot

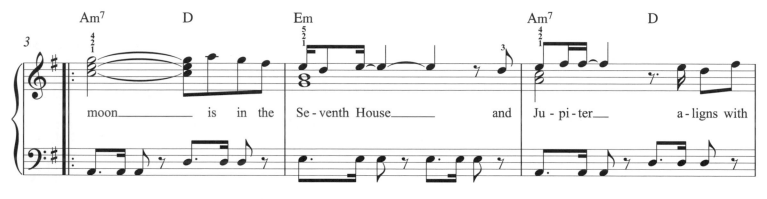

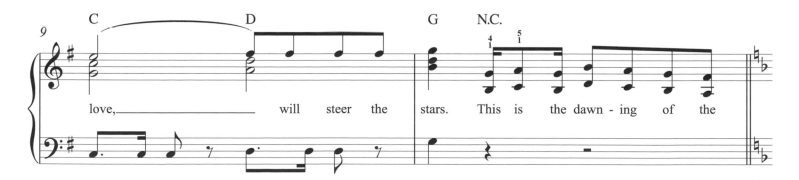

3

true li - be - ra - tion. A - qua - ri - us!

1.

— A - qua - ri - us! When the

2.

-qua - ri - us! A - qua - ri - us!

— A - qua - ri - us! A -

-qua - ri - us!

Manchester, England

Words by James Rado & Gerome Ragni
Music by Galt MacDermot

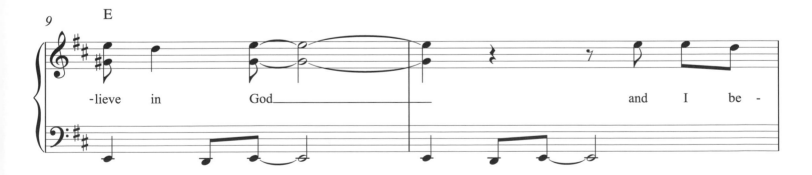

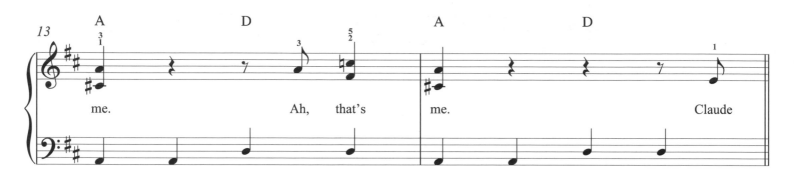

-lieve that God_____ be - lieves in Claude,_____ that's

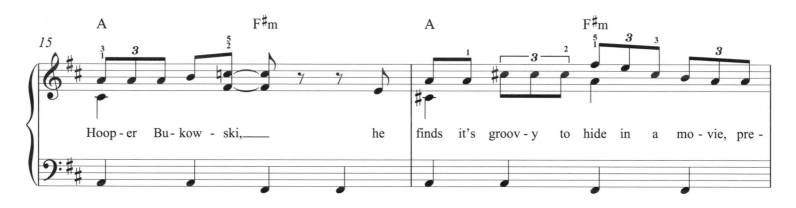

me.   Ah,   that's   me.   Claude

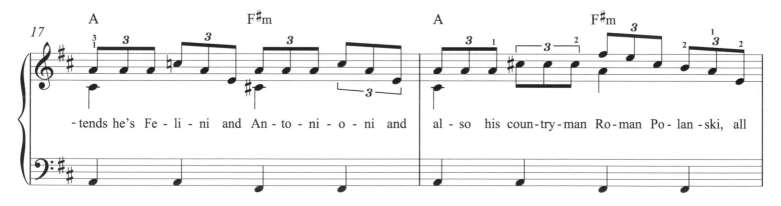

Hoop - er Bu - kow - ski,_____   he   finds it's groov - y to hide in a mo - vie, pre -

-tends he's Fe - li - ni and An - to - ni - o - ni and   al - so his coun - try - man Ro - man Po - lan - ski, all

rolled in - to one.   One Claude Hoop - er Bu - kow - ski._____

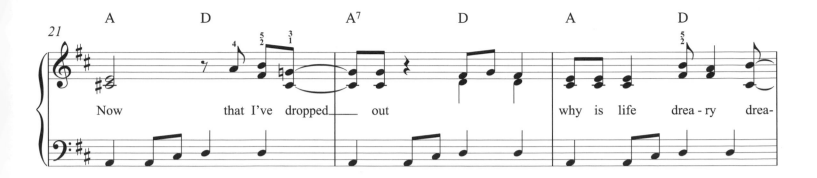

Now that I've dropped out why is life drea-ry drea-

-ry? Ans-wer my wea-ry que - ry. Whoa,

D.S. al Coda

Tim - o - thy Lea - ry, dea - rie. Oh,

Coda

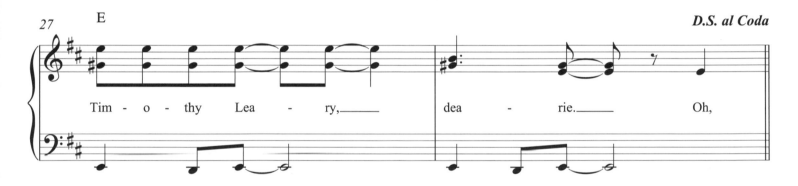

me. (That's he.) Ah, that's me. (That's he.) Ah, that's

me. (That's he.) Ah, ha ha.

Donna

Words by James Rado & Gerome Ragni
Music by Galt MacDermot

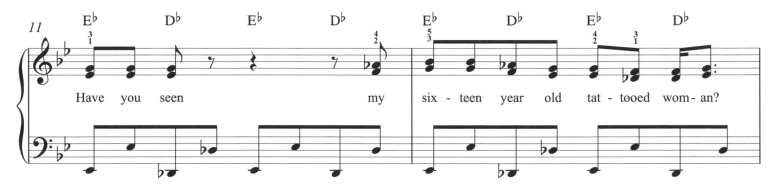

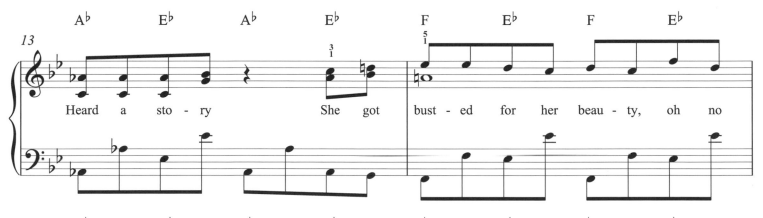

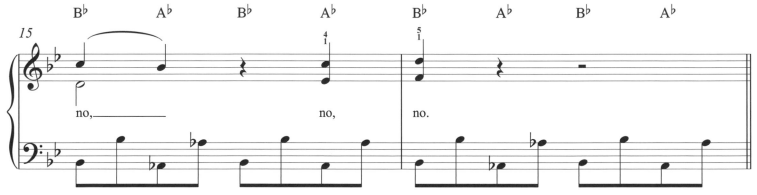

Oh, Don - na, oh oh, Don - na, oh oh oh, look - ing for my Don - na.___

I've been to In - di - a and saw the Yo - gi light.
And I'm gon - na show her that life on earth can be sweet.

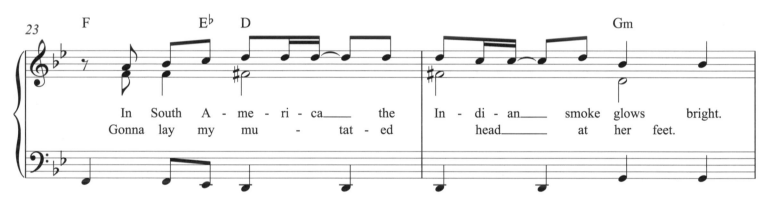

In South A - me - ri - ca___ the In - di - an___ smoke glows bright.
Gonna lay my mu - tat - ed head___ at her feet.

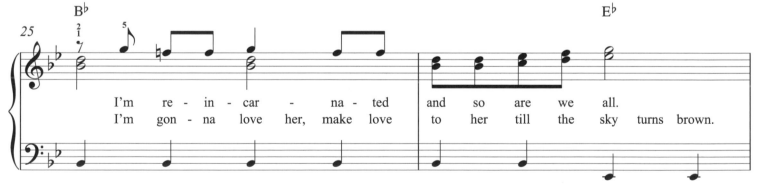

I'm re - in - car - na - ted and so are we all.
I'm gon - na love her, make love to her till the sky turns brown.

1.

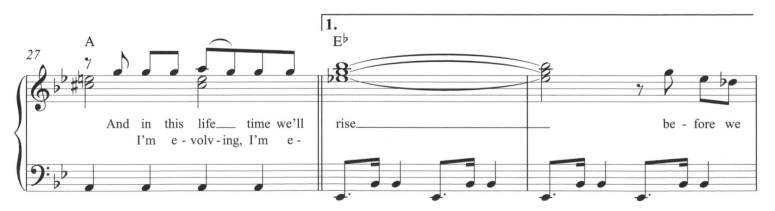

And in this life___ time we'll rise___ be - fore we
I'm e - volv - ing, I'm e -

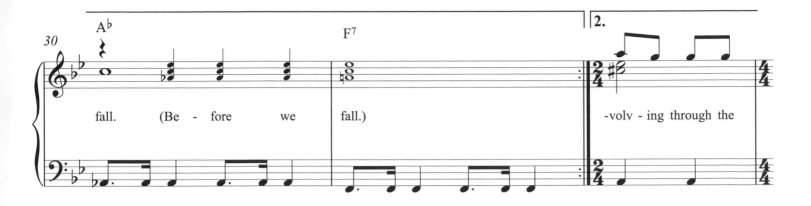

fall. (Be - fore we fall.) -volv - ing through the

drugs that you put down. (That you put

D.S. al Coda **Coda**

down.)

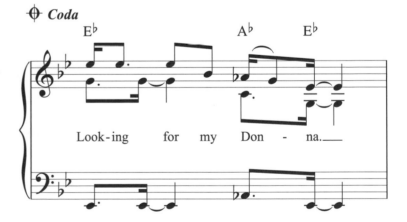

Look - ing for my Don - na.___

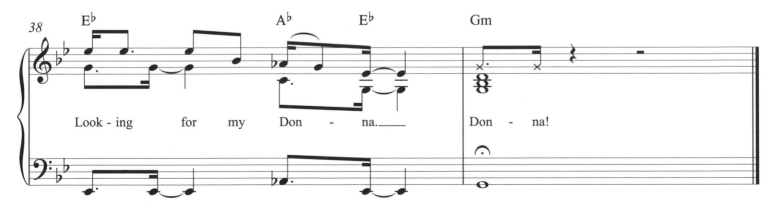

Look - ing for my Don - na.___ Don - na!

Air

Words by James Rado & Gerome Ragni
Music by Galt MacDermot

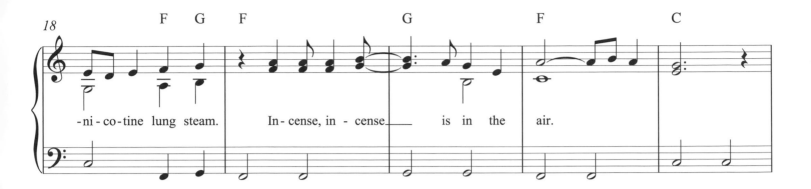

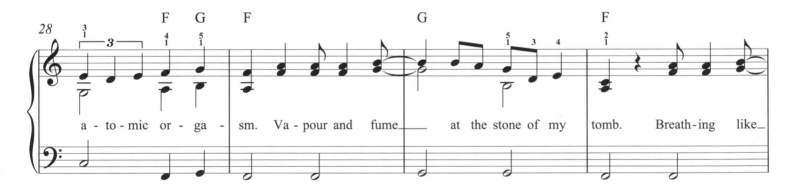

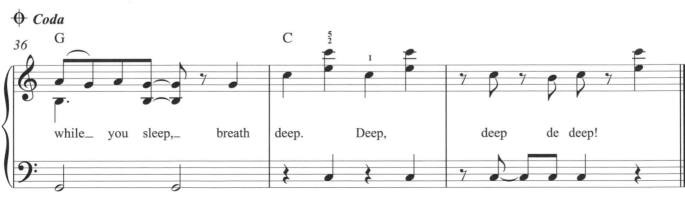

13

I'm Black/Ain't Got No

Words by James Rado & Gerome Ragni
Music by Galt MacDermot

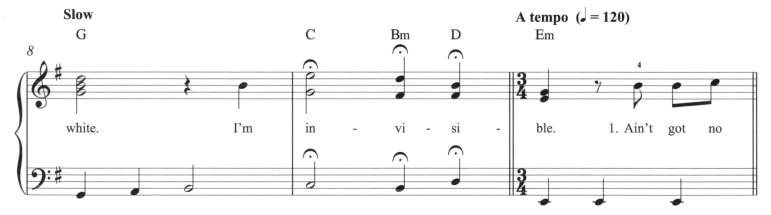

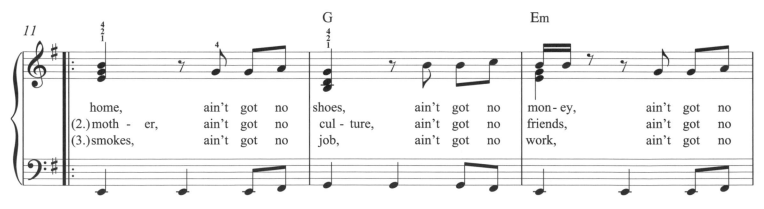

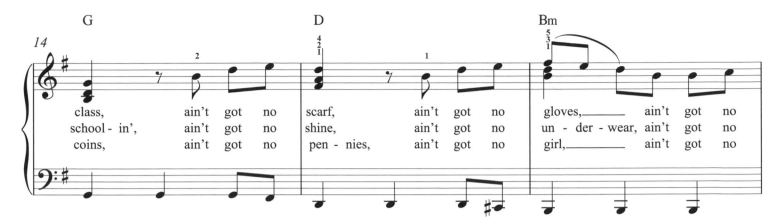

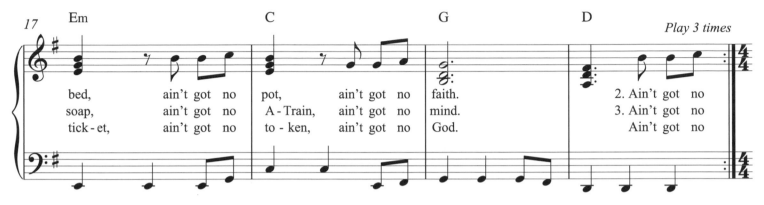

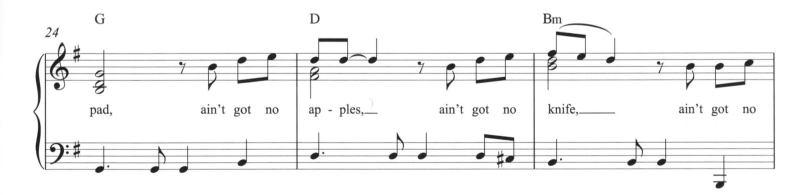

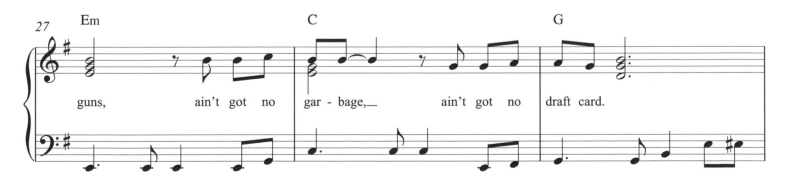

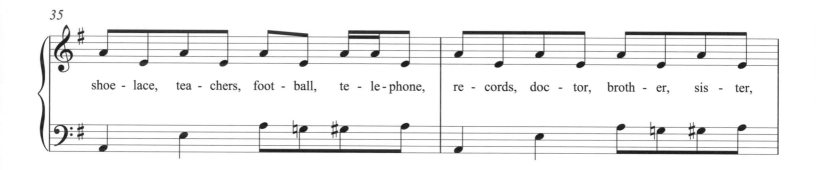

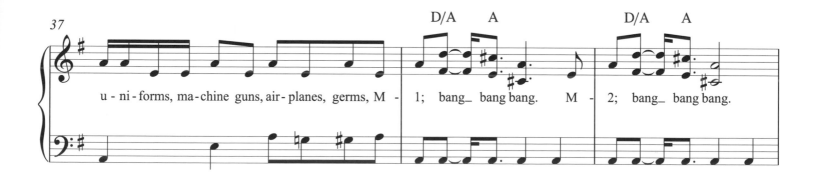

16

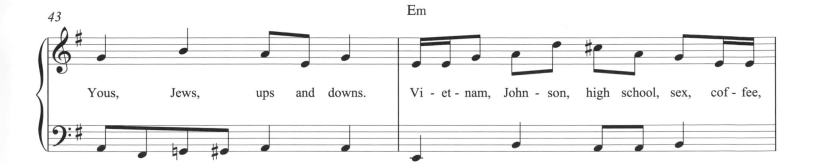

Yous, Jews, ups and downs. Vi - et - nam, John - son, high school, sex, cof - fee,

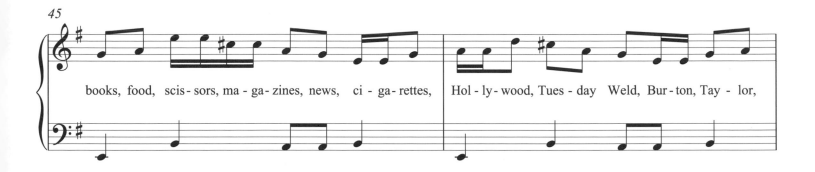

books, food, scis - sors, ma - ga - zines, news, ci - ga - rettes, Hol - ly - wood, Tues - day Weld, Bur - ton, Tay - lor,

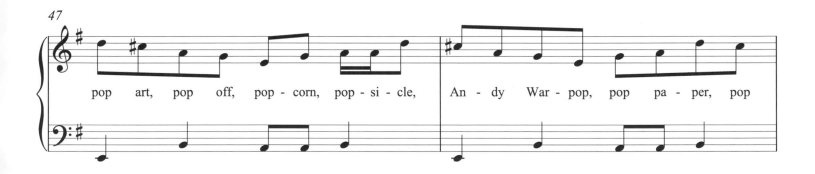

pop art, pop off, pop - corn, pop - si - cle, An - dy War - pop, pop pa - per, pop

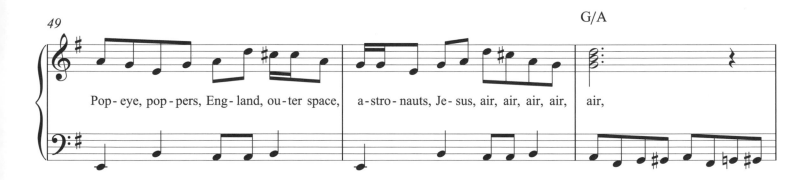

Pop - eye, pop - pers, Eng - land, ou - ter space, a - stro - nauts, Je - sus, air, air, air, air, air,

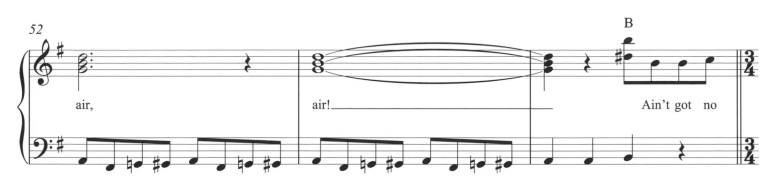

air, air!_____ Ain't got no

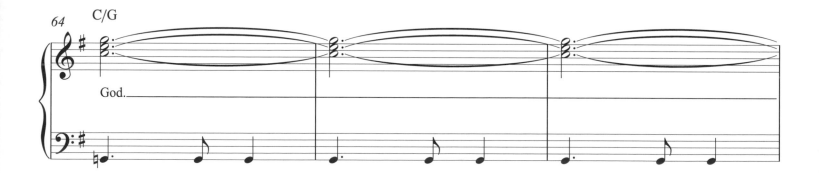

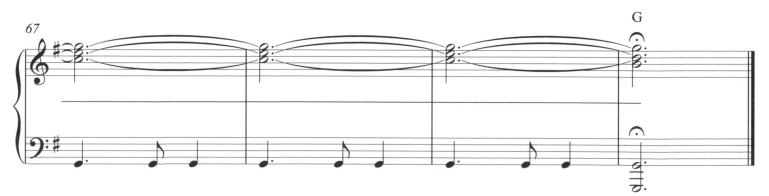

18

I Got Life

Words by James Rado & Gerome Ragni
Music by Galt MacDermot

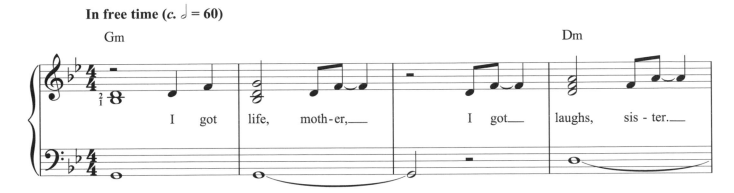

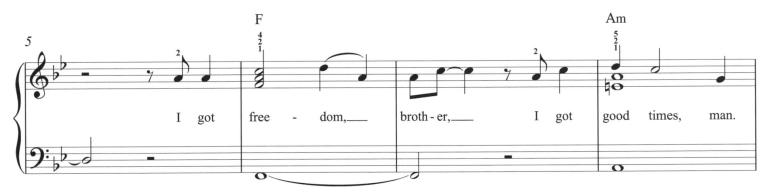

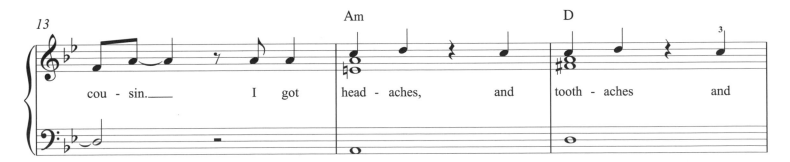

bad times too,____ like you. I got my

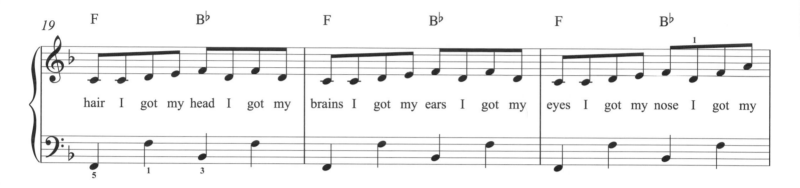

hair I got my head I got my brains I got my ears I got my eyes I got my nose I got my

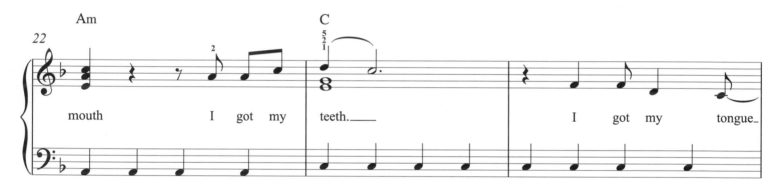

mouth I got my teeth.____ I got my tongue____

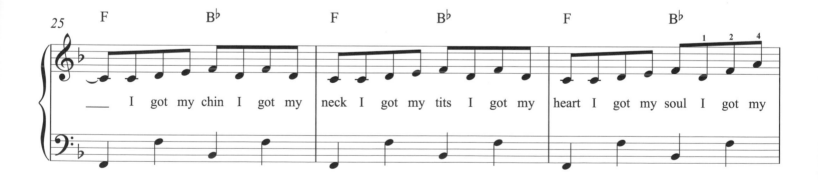

____ I got my chin I got my neck I got my tits I got my heart I got my soul I got my

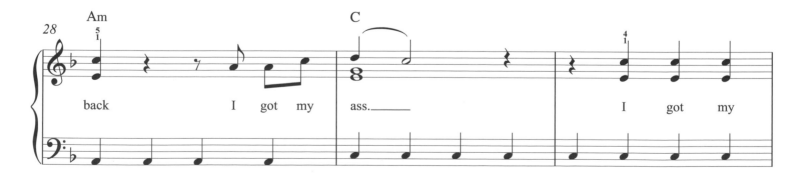

back I got my ass.____ I got my

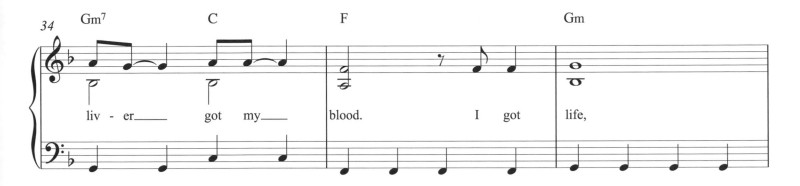

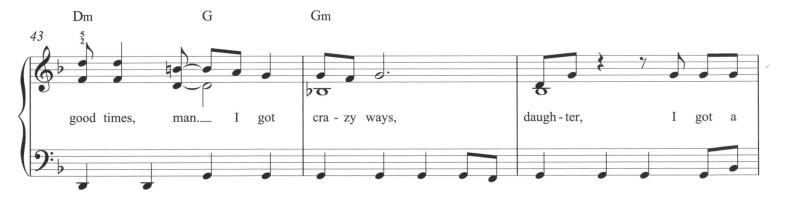

mil - lion dol - lar charm, cou - sin.___ I got head-aches and tooth-aches and

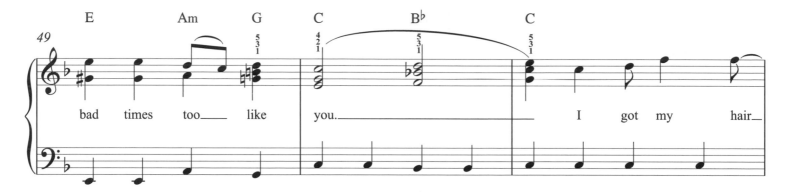

bad times too___ like you.___ I got my hair___

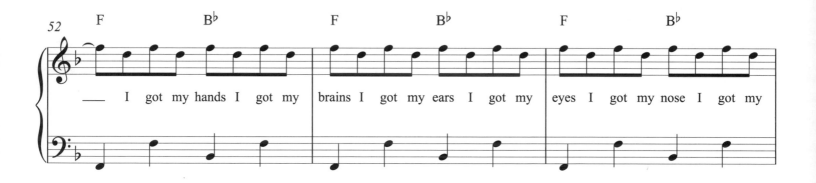

___ I got my hands I got my brains I got my ears I got my eyes I got my nose I got my

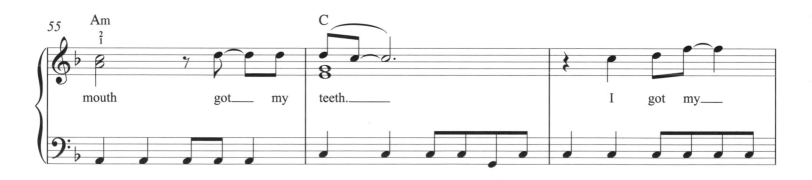

mouth got___ my teeth.___ I got my___

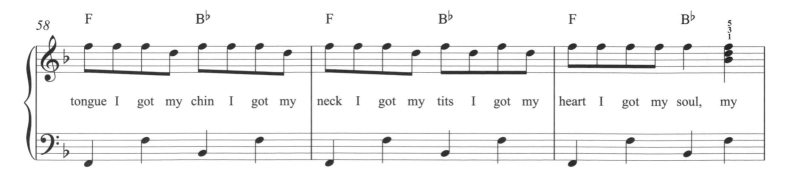

tongue I got my chin I got my neck I got my tits I got my heart I got my soul, my

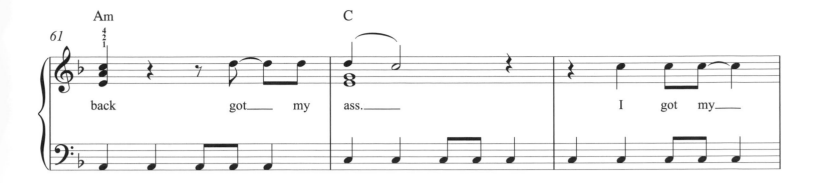

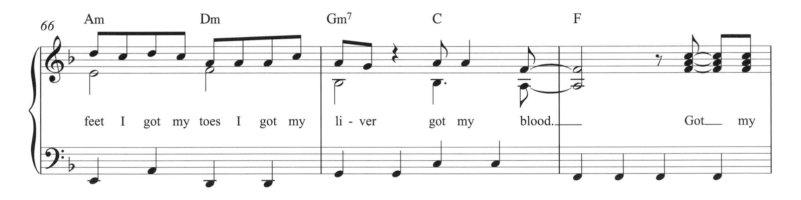

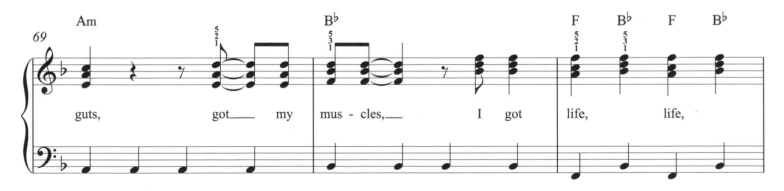

23

Hair

Words by James Rado & Gerome Ragni
Music by Galt MacDermot

25

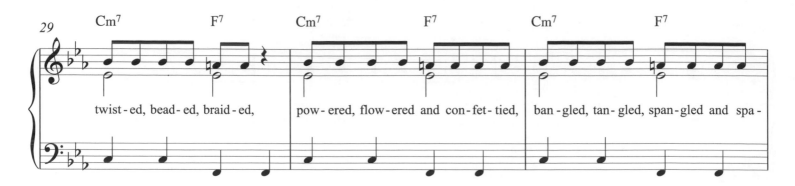

twist-ed, bead-ed, braid-ed,   pow-ered, flow-ered and con-fet-tied,   ban-gled, tan-gled, span-gled and spa-

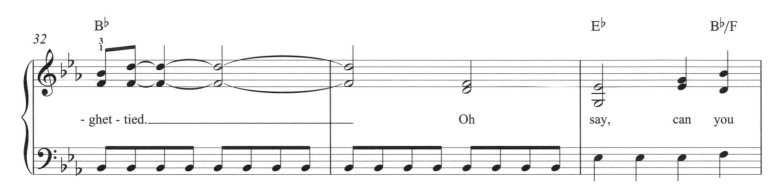

-ghet-tied._____   Oh   say,   can   you

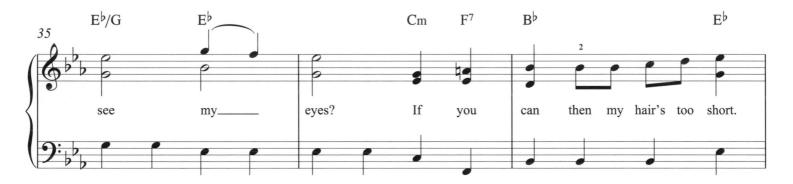

see   my_____   eyes?   If   you   can   then my hair's too short.

Down to here, down to there,   down to there, down to where it   stops by it-self.   (Do do do do

do do do do do do do do do do do   do do do do do   do.)   They'll be   ga - ga   at the go - go when they

26

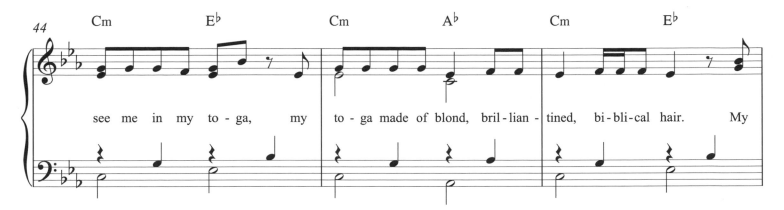

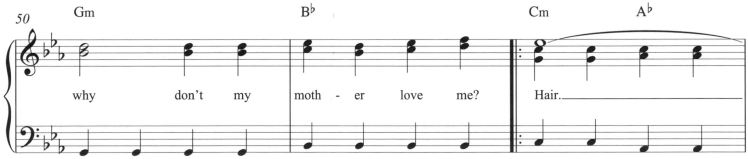

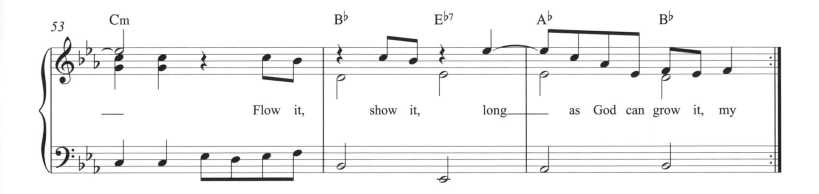

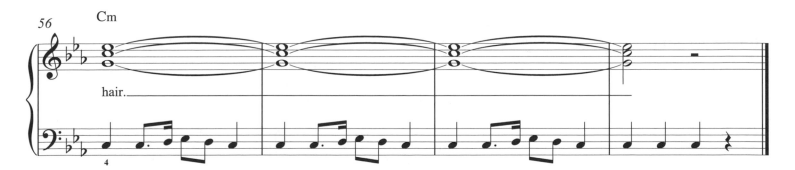

Frank Mills

Words by James Rado & Gerome Ragni
Music by Galt MacDermot

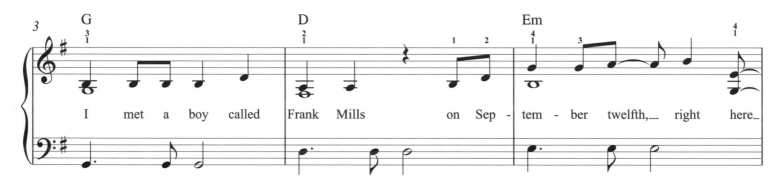

I met a boy called Frank Mills on Sep - tem - ber twelfth,___ right here___

___ in front of the Wa - ver - ley. But un - for - tu - nate - ly___

I lost his ad - dress. He was last seen with his

friend, a drum-mer; he re - sem-bles George Har - ri - son of____ The Bea - tles, but

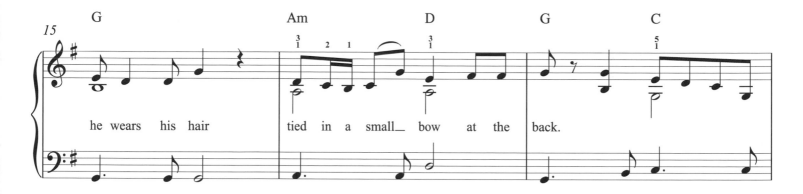

he wears his hair tied in a small__ bow at the back.

I love him, but it em - ba - ras - ses me____ to

walk down the street with him.__ He lives in Brook - lyn____

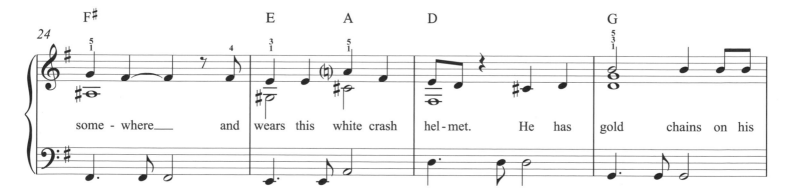

some - where____ and wears this white crash hel - met. He has gold chains on his

29

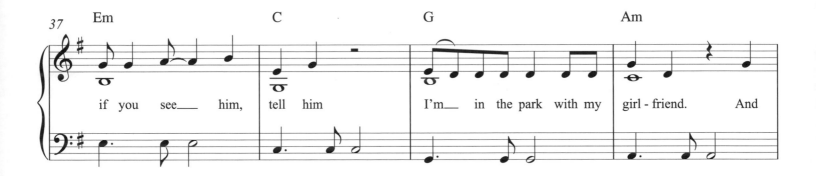

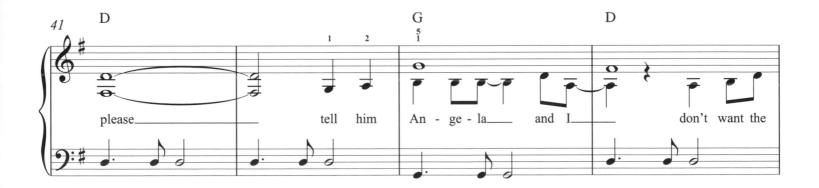

Where Do I Go?

Words by James Rado & Gerome Ragni
Music by Galt MacDermot

Fol-low the wind song,— fol-low the thun-der.— Fol-low the ne - on in

young lov-ers' eyes. Down to the gut - ter,— up to the glit - ter—

in - to the cit - y— where the truth lies.

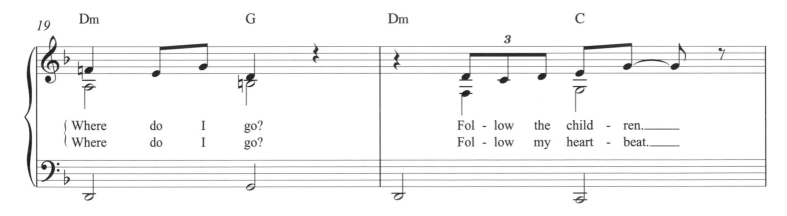

Where do I go?
Where do I go?
Fol - low the child - ren.—
Fol - low my heart - beat.—

Where do I go?— Fol-low their smiles. Is there an ans - wer
Where do I go? Fol-low my hand. Where do they lead me

in their sweet fac - es_____ that tells me why I live and die?_____
and will I ev - er_____ dis - cov - er why I live and

(Why?)_____ I live and die?_____ (Why?)_____ Do_____ I

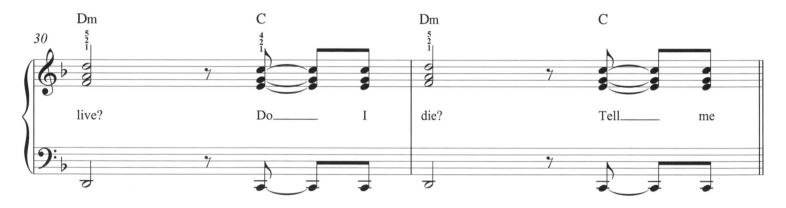

live? Do_____ I die? Tell_____ me

where_____ do_____ I go? Tell_____ me why? Tell_____ me

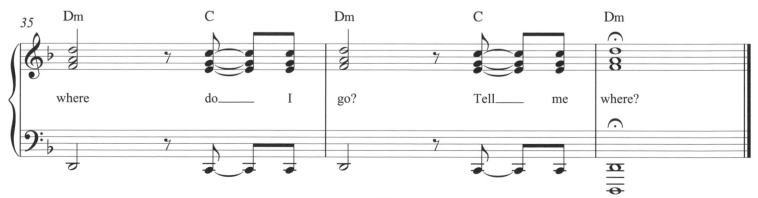

where_____ do_____ I go? Tell_____ me where?

Black Boys/White Boys

Words by James Rado & Gerome Ragni
Music by Galt MacDermot

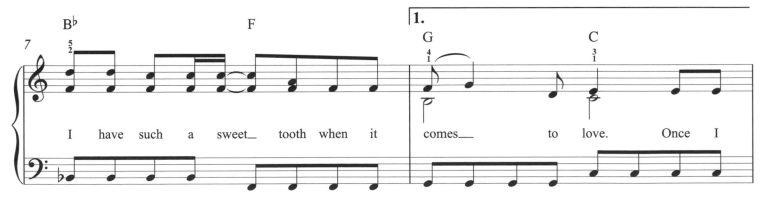

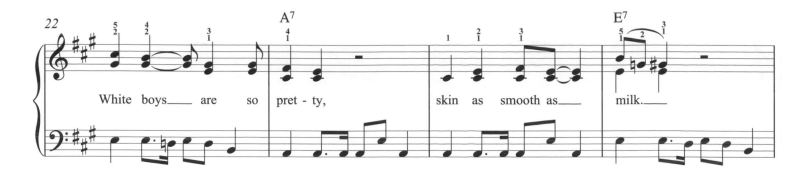

White boys___ are so pret-ty, skin as smooth as___ milk.___

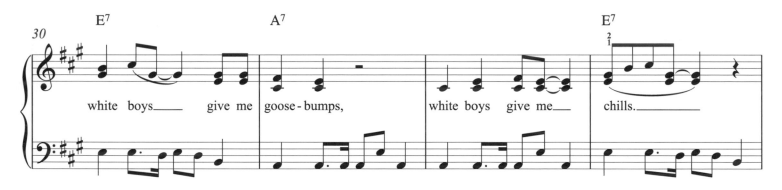

White boys are so pret-ty,___ got hair like Chi-nese___ silk. I tell you that the

white boys___ give me goose-bumps, white boys give me___ chills.___

When they touch my shoul - der that's the touch that___ kills.___ Well,__ my

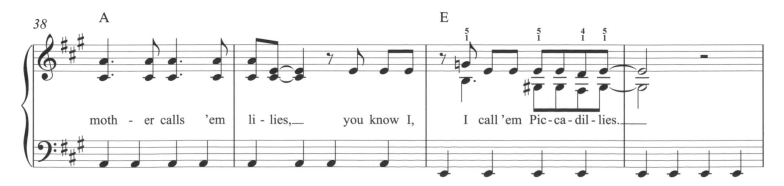

moth - er calls 'em li - lies,___ you know I, I call 'em Pic-ca-dil-lies.___

And when my dad-dy tells me "Stay a - way"_____ I just say "Come on out an'

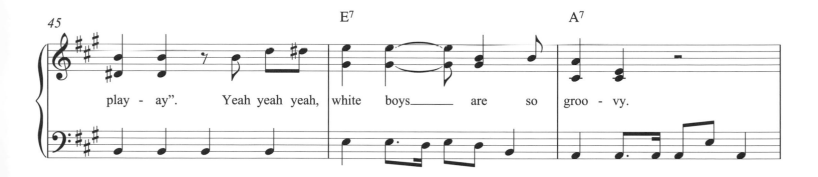

play - ay". Yeah yeah yeah, white boys_____ are so groo - vy.

White boys are so_____ tough._____ And ev-'ry time that they're

near_____ me, I just can't get e - nough.

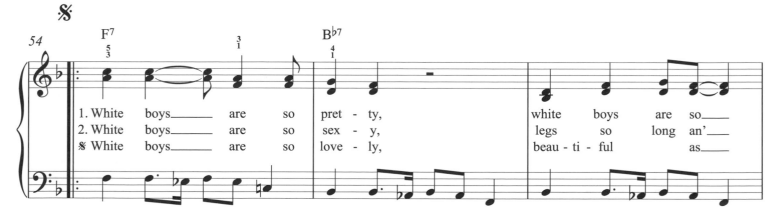

1. White boys_____ are so pret - ty, white boys are so_____
2. White boys_____ are so sex - y, legs so long an'_____
% White boys_____ are so love - ly, beau - ti - ful as_____

37

sweet._____ White boys drive me cra - - zy,
lean._____ I love those sprayed - on trou - - sers,
girls._____ I love to run my___ fin - - gers

1.

they drive me in - dis - creet._____
I love the love ma - chine._____
an' toes, through all their curls._____

To Coda ⊕

2.

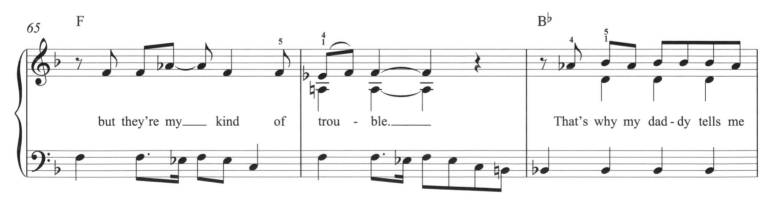

Well,__ my broth - er calls 'em rub - ble,___

but they're my__ kind of trou - ble._____ That's why my dad - dy tells me

D.S. al Coda

"No, no, no,___ no"__ I just say "whites boys go,__ go go,__ go, go, go".

38

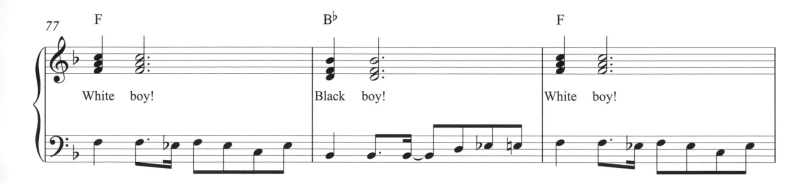

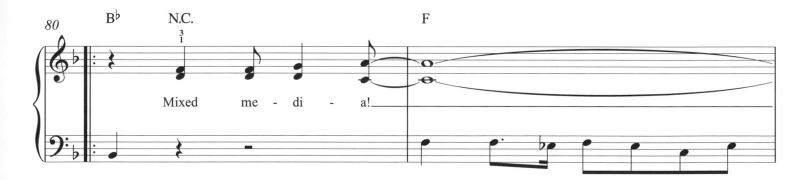

39

Easy To Be Hard

Words by James Rado & Gerome Ragni
Music by Galt MacDermot

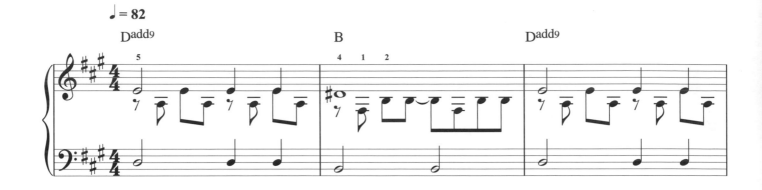

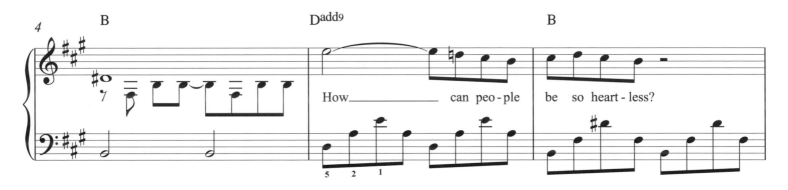

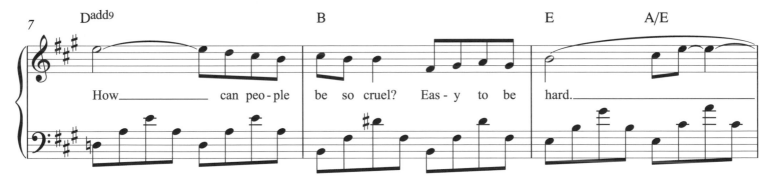

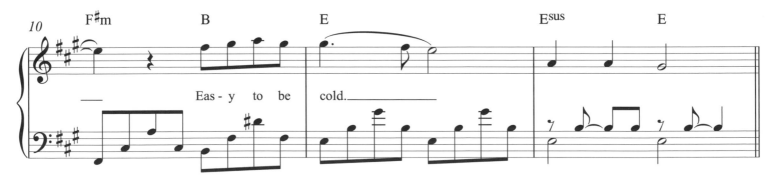

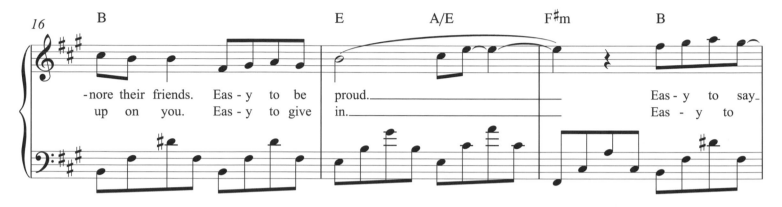

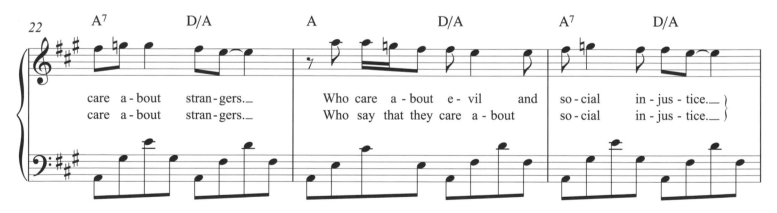

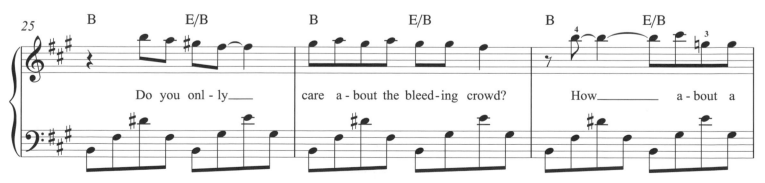

41

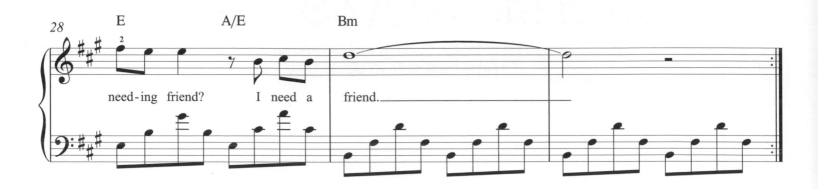

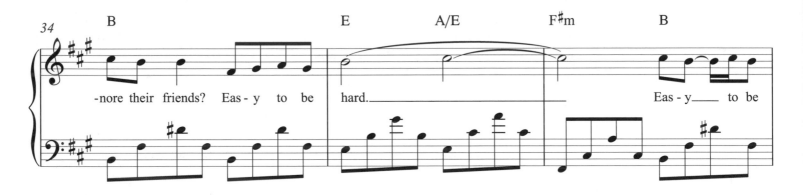

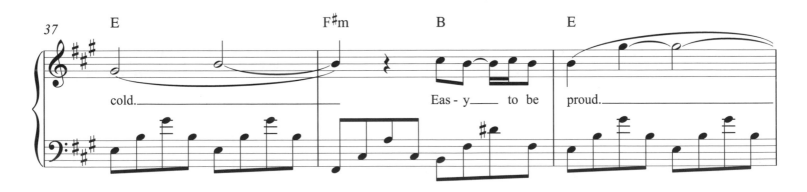

Good Morning Starshine

Words by James Rado & Gerome Ragni
Music by Galt MacDermot

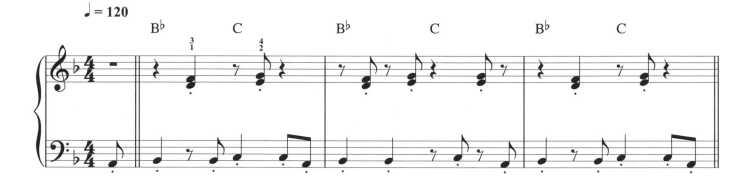

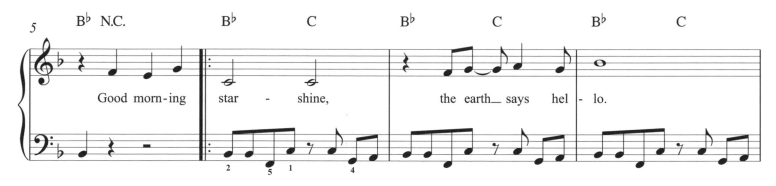

Good morn-ing star - shine, the earth__ says hel - lo.

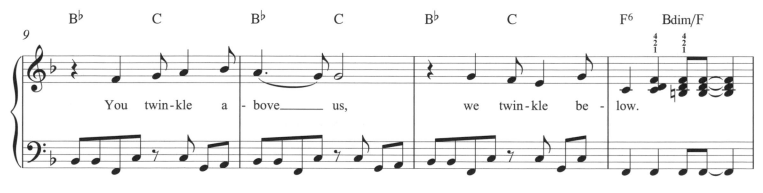

You twin-kle a - bove_____ us, we twin-kle be - low.

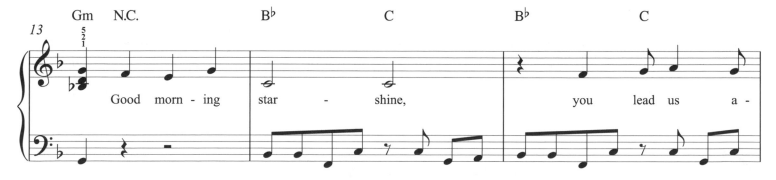

Good morn - ing star - shine, you lead us a -

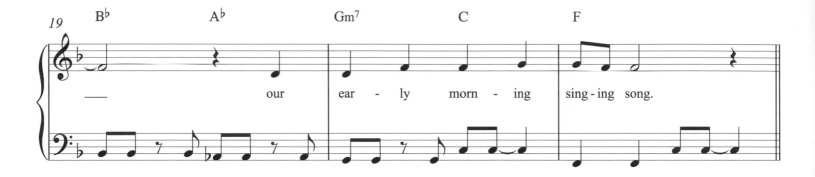

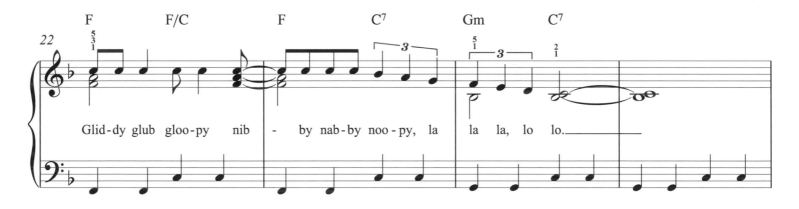

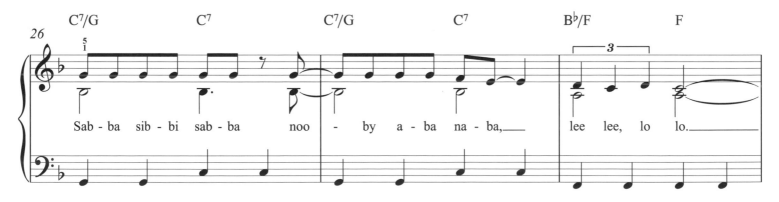

44

The Flesh Failures/
Let The Sunshine In

Words by James Rado & Gerome Ragni
Music by Galt MacDermot

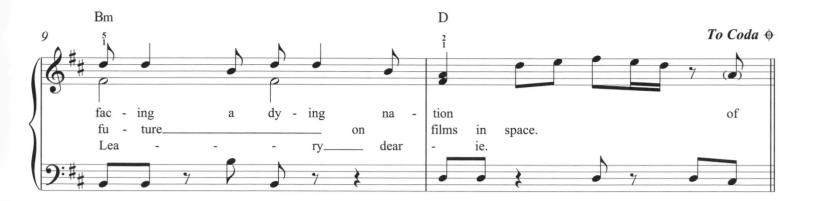

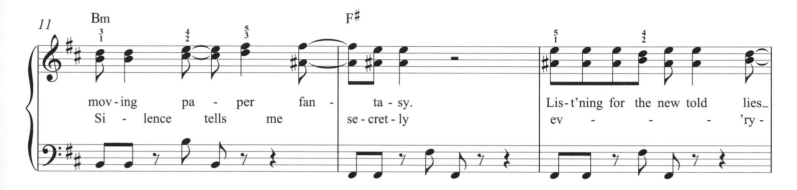

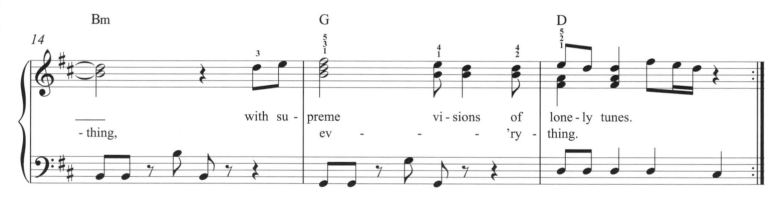

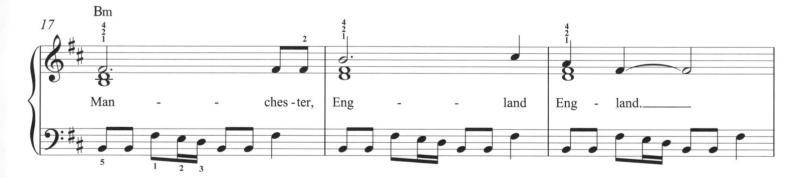

-cross   the At-lan-tic   Sea.___   And   I'm   a ge-nius, ge - nius,___   I___ be-

-lieve   in___ God___   and I be - lieve   that___ God be - lieves   in___ Claude, that's

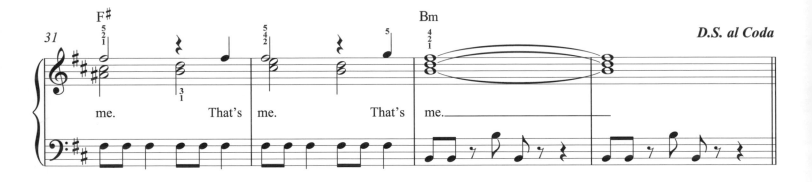

me.   That's me.   That's   me.___

D.S. al Coda

$\oplus$ *Coda*

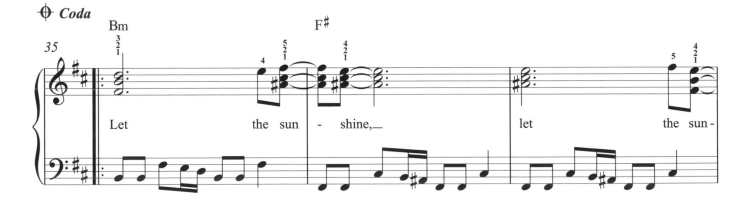

Let   the sun - shine,___   let   the sun-

-shine in,___   the   sun - - shine   in.

Repeat to fade

123456789